A Blessing in the Midst of Darkness

by

Melanie Antonia

A Blessing in the Midst of Darkness

Copyright © by Author: Melanie Antonia, 2023

Cover Illustration by: Dylan Fernandez

The right of Melanie Antonia to be identified legally as Author of this work has been asserted in accordance with sections 77 and 78 of the Copyright, Designs and Patents Act, 1988.

Published by: Melanie Antonia Fernandez, London, 2023
With the service of: TamaRe House, UK
044 (0) 844 357 2592, www.tamarehouse.com

ISBN: 978-1-7395513-1-5

This publication uses archival-quality paper

A CIP record of this publication is available from the British Library.

A Blessing in the Midst of Darkness

Contents

Acknowledgements 7

A Mother's Love 8

For my baby girl...................................9

A leader 11

Your strength within 13

Home..14

The journey that awaits you 16

Onwards to greatness............................17

A message to you all.............................19

Standing united as one 21

A picture speaks many words, actions speak a thousand 22

When the end has finally come 23

Standing stronger than ever! 24

The truth exposed 25

A positive outlook................................26

Never a failure 27

A blessing on its way 28

Rebuilding to become 29

Somewhere along the way 30

When a new day comes 32

Jealousy or Love 34

Happiness Is 37

Your heart is truth 39

A Moment Alone 41

A woman 43

The smile 45

To believe in the unseen 46

The man for me 48

A moment to reflect 49

Observe 51

Encourage 52

The end 53

Marriage 54

Affirmation 55

Hurt 56

For a moment 57

Covid world 58

Grace 59

Gratitude 60

A Christmas reflection 61

Hurting 63

Imperfect...64

Unknown 66

Confirmation 67

Grace & mercy.....................................68

Positive progress 69

Movement..70

Godly encounter...................................72

Faithfulness 73

Believing 74

The vision 75

Rising 76

Acknowledgements

Without pain there is no healing, without loss there is no appreciation for life, without purpose we feel empty.

I give thanks to God, with undoubted faith. My testimony, is how I was saved at the nearest point of death and this will be my story. I want to thank my sons, Shane and Dylan for their unconditional love, through our toughest years and for believing in my potential and growth, even when I didn't - they never gave up on me.

Thank you to my partner, Lyndon, who has given me our daughter, Ellysia-Grace. God's favour. Finally, I want to thank everyone who has passed through my life. At some point your encounter has inspired me to reflect and grow.

1 Corinthians 13:13 - So now faith, hope, and love abide, these three; but the greatest of these is love!

A Mother's Love

A mother's love when I first looked at you,

gave me an overwhelming feeling, I was unsure of what to do.

The blessing that came upon my life, I knew nothing more could be taken in my stride.

God has given me a gift, a gift which is you, son so precious and delicate to.

The love for you is unconditional and with my last breath, although sounds traditional.

I will give my all and try my utmost best,

to make sure you only, ever need rest.

Remember that I, will always love you,

because I know in my heart that you love me too!

My sons,

Shane & Dylan xx

For my baby girl

Before you are born, I want to write this letter,

because my wish for you is that your life is better.

Better than the start that I had in mine,

so I am planting roots so you can be the vine.

Around us are many who will seem to be excited,

but with discernment we will know they are actually divided.

When you are born people will come and go,

some will be friends and some will be foes.

Our job is to protect you, love and nurture you,

so your life will be one, that goes further.

You are our gift that we waited for so long,

carrying you warmly, makes me feel so strong.

That no matter what life brings our way,

the love that surrounds you, will always make you stay.

Stay close to us, your family entwined,

you are the destiny that is destined to shine.

The love I feel for you is pure and true,

I can't wait for the day when I get to hold you.

For now, though, I will enjoy the time that I carry,

before I know you will be here in a hurry.

I love you baby girl and always will.

My precious, my beauty forever until.

Love you Ellysia-Grace x

A leader

A leader at the forefront whom I admire and respect,

we know she has our best interest's least we do not forget.

Admiring her strength and beauty as a woman she stands strong against it all,

we are there, to ensure nothing makes her fall.

Taking this opportunity to thank her for bringing us this far, we cannot do it alone, she is our shining star.

So often we are caught up, in our own battles and strife, acknowledge the wisdom she brings and humble in our lives.

Whatever life throws at us, we must stand up against it, set apart from each other we are far from being misfits.

The uniqueness you have brought to our community, is much to be admired,

keep pressing forward and alight your burning fire

She welcomes the children with her friendly smile,

and reassures them of their abilities, all of the while.

They care so much of her own wellbeing, and miss
her presence around,

when they see her at the school door, they feel safe,
secure and sound.

Thank you Carol x

Your strength within

Amidst all the chaos you always displayed a smile,

a women of integrity, seeing the good in everyone around.

Encouraging the children, the best that they can be.

Instilling order, calmness and lots of fun to create their security.

We owe to you the recent success, as you gave nothing but your ultimate best.

Always be proud of the trials that you faced, as this was the reason you were placed, in the school that needed a professional touch, to carry us through the clear mis-judge.

The mis-judge of potential our children have to offer, in the community, where no one else bothers.

Gratitude and respect will always be for you, as you were the one, who helped my dreams come true.

Thank you Sarah S x

Home

I feel so lonely I want to go home
I feel so alone in this cold empty room.

I feel so lonely isolated from this world
I am all alone – there is no one here.
I want to be home where I feel alive,
I want to see walls, that bring back life.
I have my own thoughts, yet I have no voice,
I feel so lonely, I want to go home.
I want to laugh again and see the smallest of bugs
I want to feel loved again and have the tightest of hugs.

My little robin friend, alone in the garden,
waiting for sound... but all around there is silence.
I feel so lonely, I want to go home
I feel so alone, my voice no longer I own.
I feel so lonely, I want to go home,

A Blessing in the Midst of Darkness

To where I belong… the place I call home.

My bestie Rob x

The journey that awaits you

<u>Class 6 of 2020</u>

The time has come for to say goodbye,

to stretch your wings and learn to fly.

The memories we've made,

we'll treasure so dear,

The road at the moment in front of you,

may somewhat seem unclear.

Thank you for the laughter and the joyful tears,

hold onto the skills you've learnt...

and you'll have nothing to fear.

The journey that awaits you is full of new adventure,

recognise your potential and embrace all the ventures.

It's left for me to wish you, all the very best,

loving yourself in every moment and you'll stand out from the rest.

Special love and God bless you always x

A Blessing in the Midst of Darkness

Onwards to greatness

Class 6 of 2022

Onwards to greatness, now you shall go,

for your time in primary school has been sown.

You have left an imprint on all of our hearts,

now it's time to make a start.

Make a start on your destiny, that now awaits you,

for every decision you make, will surely guide you.

Be strong, be courageous and do not follow,

for you have all been gifted with greatness not sorrow.

The best advice I will leave you with,

is stay true to yourself, have fun and live.

Opportunities await you, grab them with both hands,

do not hesitate, but rather make a stand.

A final note before we say goodbye,

soar like eagles, aim high and fly.

Remember these words and keep them close to your heart,

for the goodness you have, will never depart x

A Blessing in the Midst of Darkness

A message to you all

<u>Class 6 of 2023</u>

As I wrote this poem for all of you to hear,

I'm not gonna lie, I shed a few tears.

My first teaching class during the period of lockdown,

we stronger together and never once did we backdown.

It has been a pleasure to watch you all flourish,

into fine young adults which memories I will cherish.

My last words to you before you leave,

is remind yourselves each day, you can achieve.

Believe with your resilience and all that you have acquired,

that you will excel in all you desire.

Follow your dreams and leave your mark,

none of you were born to stay in the dark.

But rather to shine and never grow tired,

instead, be those that continually inspire.

I will miss you all, it goes without saying,

Melanie Antonia

but remember your journey starts now, with no delaying.

Stay safe, stay blessed and know in your heart,

God will do the rest and provide a fresh start x

Standing united as one

As we stand united showing our love,

where the world comes together gathering like doves.

Doves of hope and doves of peace,

caring for each other removing judgement and disbelief.

Our heroes they surface, in times of our needs,

saving one's souls and sowing like seeds.

Seeds for our future and new beginnings to come,

where countries stand united and prosper as one.

A picture speaks many words, actions speak a thousand

Loving someone, is more than temporary lust,

it comes together, with forgiveness and trust.

Their softest touch, their unique fragrance,

their sweetest kiss, beauty and patience.

The balance they bring to your ultimate being,

fulfils your purpose and manifests your believing.

Believing in your potential, to eternally shine,

like the brightest star and becoming the spine.

The spine that through storms, that does not wither,

but staying uprooted and keeping together.

Reaching beyond, as far as the stars,

ashes to beauty with no visible scars.

The man, the king, who holds your crown,

is the one who will garment you in a golden gown.

When the end has finally come

This is it, the moment is here,

what I've dreaded for time and all that I feared.

Saying goodbye to the one I've truly loved,

but no more can we carry on, even though I've called
on the above.

I pray for peace, I pray for calm,

I can't move forward alone, for I will miss his charm.

We can no longer continue, that we both know,

unfortunately for him, he simply cannot show.

The respect I want and the respect I deserve,
unconditional and truthful, with no hesitation or
reserve.

I wanted him forever, I wanted him for life,

but all that reoccurs is heartache and strife.

Saying goodbye is the hardest thing to do,

all that I felt for him, will always be true.

Standing stronger than ever!

From this day forward I will not look back,

the war within me, wants me to go off track.

If I look back 24 hours, when I wanted to end my life,

it seems as though, God has renewed my strife.

Giving me cause and purpose, not to live in vain,

but to move on and flourish, forgetting all the pain.

The pain that confused and corrupted my mind, will not take residence, in my new design.

I believe I was made for better, I believe that this is true,

'Keep pressing forward' God speaks 'I will get you through'.

Be strong and resilient to what is coming your way, be sure to guard your heart, so that you will not feel mislaid.

From this day onwards, I will endeavour to grow,

and in the hearts of those who know me, I will love, prosper and sow.

A Blessing in the Midst of Darkness

The truth exposed

The heart can lie,

but the gut never denies.

To the feelings inside,

that try to disguise.

What the other heart feels,

and the hurt that it reels,

when one discovers the truth,

you could feel all aloof.

But then wisdom steps in,

and your inner power begins.

Value yourself and what you have to offer,

before you know, the insecurity will make you feel lower.

That is not your path, that is not where you should go

be true in who you are and then you will know,

your beauty that shines is what will eventually grow.

A positive outlook

A positive outlook brings a positive mind,

with opportunities around us, we will be amazed with what we find.

Searching high and searching low,

life will take us on a journey, that is all but slow.

Like a rollercoaster at its peak,

Sometimes we are silent, sometimes we speak.

You must hold the bar with both hands, be sure to stay on top and control where you land.

Where you land is where you discover,

your purpose in life for you to uncover.

The beauty you hold and project to others,

Never failing to see as a gifted mother,

all that you have done is for another.

The light you possess, will keep on shining through,

let everyone who you see, know that you are true.

Never a failure

Love yourself with all your heart,

by doing this you will set yourself apart.

Your road you are taking is yours alone,

don't be afraid to challenge and make it your own.

You have come so far, through obstacles and pain,

only you and you alone, can reap in the gain.

You are not a failure, this you must know,

God has blessed you with so much, and that is why
we love him so.

A blessing on its way

That moment, when hope resides in your soul,

the mind speaks to your heart and even closer to your goal.

Within your grasp, these decisions evidently lie,

no more can you deny, the excitement in your eyes.

The feeling of success, brightens each step that you take,

for your newfound confidence, in the past mistakes.

Can doubt your achievement and what's coming your way,

trusting in God, is all you can say.

All the struggles and pain that we had to face,

is merely God's way of revealing his grace.

Bountiful beauty he bestows on our face,

no make-up is evident - just a natural face.

Where you go from here, already has God's hand,

he will set you on a path - to what will be your promise land.

Rebuilding to become

Another day over, another day complete,

all the dramas and challenges faced, are now far beneath my feet.

Opening my eyes to the world that moves around me,

I realise more than ever that I Myself, is set free.

Set free from the torment and burden of life's disguise,

That once laid rest upon my troubled mind.

Now I can be confident to reach my goal,

The goal that is now set within my sights- realising now, it won't be such a fight!

Somewhere along the way

My heart has struggled and still remains,

what is hurt and what is pain,

when going through it, there's little gain.

The gain you get is the lesson learnt,

rather than the scars you earnt.

The tears I've cried, continue to flow,

like a speeding waterfall, continuing to grow.

My heart is love but my heart is hurt,

like someone has tossed it into the dirt.

Tainted with fear and very little trust,

any trust I do appear to have, quickly turns to dust.

This frustration needs to end and a solution to be
sort,

after all you have one life,

and life we know is short.

Let him go to find his way,

because if he's not yours, then he will not stay.

Furthermore, the two of us are hurting,
one day it may explode - then was it worth waiting.
Loving him is not enough thirst,
trusting him has to come first.
I pray for this confusion, to come good in the end,
for in this love, I have for him - I will defend.

When a new day comes

When a new day comes it's like a revelation,

too many mistakes, made along the way to bring hesitation.

Hesitation, for the what if,

if the what if was always there, how can we say life is not fair.

Trusting in God with all your might,

so that he can take over and win the fight.

The battle is not yours, says the Lord,

so don't become complacent and do not get bored.

A new day has been given and now we can be driven,

by the road that lies ahead,

so we are reborn, not dead.

Thank you, Lord, for the blessings upon me,

A Blessing in the Midst of Darkness

give me grace and mercy, so that others will see me.

See me and know your love,

Then they will believe that you are, forever above.

Jealousy or Love

The two components and emotions,

can eventually lead to a lethal potion.

It is death at its doors, if the other wants more and

no one can see it coming.

When love is there,

there is no need for fear.

But if the path is made,

then the future is laid.

Laid out ahead,

which can leave you for dead.

Struggling for breath,

Struggling for life,

all you want to be, is the profound and perfect wife.

How can you be? When jealousy is what you see,

You don't choose these emotions they choose you.

Like a fine wine off a dusty shelf,

you were doing so well and even your health.

But then you lose your glow,

and now nobody knows.

How you have changed,

and they remain the same.

Crying and crying floods the eyes,

your fed up with all the cheated lies.

All you know is fear and let down,

The men you have known, have worn the crown.

Snap out and change,

if you want to regain.

Regain your peace,

Melanie Antonia   35

regain your mind,

and then you will find love, in God's ordained time.

A Blessing in the Midst of Darkness

Happiness Is

Happiness is seeing your children achieve,

because first and foremost, they know you believe.

Believe in their strengths and their determination at that,

rewarding them favourably, revealing the fact.

Love goes beyond the words,

and with that comes, their blessings deserve.

Happiness is your partner's eyes,

that connects profoundly, as your gaze arise.

Their warm touch as you fall asleep,

knowing they are there and there for keeps.

Happiness is the success that you are,

no monetary value, can reach you that far.

Melanie Antonia

For the success that you own, is for your own
standing,

to be true to yourself, with complete understanding.

Happiness is, the people around you, and with their
joy it overwhelms you.

Your heart is truth

Deep in your heart you know,

because in time your head tells you so.

When the two combined, slowly entwine, you are on

the path to let go.

Over time you will see the flaws,

it's going nowhere, just closed shut doors

Why fight the struggle and mask the pain,

when all its for, is to go insane.

God's promise is peace and prosperity,

so don't fall victim to the hostility.

No one has the right, to inflict this much pain,

so, make sure you stand back and step out of the

rain.

Melanie Antonia

The sun shines upon the righteous,

so don't ever give up, on being valued as priceless.

If the one you're with fails to see your beauty,

hug them, wave and remove yourself... indefinitely.

A Moment Alone

A moment alone, gives time for reflection,
with a glance in the mirror, no need for perfection.

Loving who you are, is the greatest gift to oneself,
knowing that what lies ahead, is a promise in itself.

The promise of hope and finding the one,
God will bless abundantly, so his will may be done.

Thanking him daily, is what we should do,
holding onto his grace, that will bring us through.

Out of the valley and out of the darkness,
his unfailing love will surely surprise us.

Be gracious and humble in all that you do,
so God our almighty, is given precedence to shine
through.

Melanie Antonia

Thank you, Lord, for the gift you have given me,

so now in turn, I can bless others accordingly.

A woman

Intricate beauty beyond the shell,
only those who she trusts, will know her so well.

Loving herself, makes her effortlessly attractive,
with no need for a man to make her assertive.

She stands up tall with her eyes fixed to the sky,
where lays her God, in the heavens align.

No need for a man to reassure her of her worth,
but instead to realise, because of her birth.

The Lord will shower his love for her always,
and guide her steps, to protect her in all days.

Thank you to those, that love their woman
profoundly,
and teaching their wives that men have boundaries.

Be committed to such beauty and peace in front of them,

So that they never depart and will never, condemn them.

The smile

A glimpse of his smile is all that it takes,

to realise, that not everything relies on being fake.

He has sincerity in his eyes, that no one can deny,

For his charm that comes with him, is by no means disguised.

The gentleness of his character and the warmth of his presence,

that is longed for so very often, is merely just in essence.

To believe in the unseen

The word is Faith,
Faith to acknowledge God's Grace.

His grace so gentle and so mild,
with no room for emptiness or straying in the wild.

The world that awaits us with fears and flaws,
holding on to God's mercy and love, will sure open
doors.

Doors to peace and a sense of calm,
to love one another without using charm.

How God so loved the world, that he has his only
begotten son,
When he commands our emotions, that's when his
will is done.

Trusting in him with all that we have,
never doubting for one moment, his unfailing love.

Faith is to believe in the unseen,
for God's mercy and Grace, will never demean.

The man for me

The man for me shows love and compassion,
he is humble and true by following no fashion.

A Godly man who sees beauty within,
rather than the glow, from the outer skin.

A deep profound feeling which sparks my glow,
others will look and others will know.

That the man for me stands by my side,
to magnify my strengths, no matter how high.

I wait silently, for the man for me, and only I will
know, when that time will be.

A moment to reflect

As I sit, stop and pause,

it gives me opportunity to see all my cause.

The cause that occupies my burdened mind,

trying to search, but what's there to find.

I wonder at what point life changed for me,

but still, I search and cannot see.

The what ifs and what I's,

insignificant to everyone's eyes.

No one cares no one knows, too many out there just
pleasing foes,

I've turned to God so many times,

searching for answers but I fail each time.

It's hard to maintain such a perfect life,

when all around us, surrounded by lies.

The imperfect perfect is what il settle for,

s this is the comfort that brings me no war.

The war is my mind, my hopes and expectations... is this a big ask of the world? If there are no limitations.

Observe

The eyes that speak,

with no need for sound,

with eyes so gentle, it lifts u off the ground.

In the hustle and bustle of work and strain,

his look disguises his deepest pain.

With God on his side, he does not look down,

but instead raises his eyes, with no glimpse of a frown.

Days go by and so does he,

enjoying his life, which is how it should be!

Encourage

A new day has come,
we thank the Lord for his son,
Fears & anxiety will be taken away,
as his mercy is upon us, in every single way.
God will be with you when you present your speech,
through your wisdom and poetry, you will surely
teach.
The gift you are blessed with is worth more than
silver and gold,
and the effects of words, will be like a story you
unfold.

The end

The day I die,
I don't you to cry.
waiting for your love,
all I did was sigh.
Now I fly,
so, so high.
Above in the sky,
yet still I cry.

For that one guy who brought, tears to my eyes,
now I say bye and yet still I cry,
Wiping my eyes, feeling less than high.

Turning to nigh
and slowly I die... eventually saying, the last goodbye.

Marriage

The bond of marriage is more than just lust,
it bears witness, to the seal of trust.
The seal between two persons coming together,
to profess their deep love, a promise forever.
Keep God in the centre of all your burdens to follow,
your prayers will be answered, and they will not be
hollow.
Love each other with respect and care, the love
between you should always be fair.
Take each other's hands, be proud and make a stand.
Guide each other's path, so that each day is a
blessing and your children to follow, will be the
telling. Of your faithful love towards each other and
forever more grow your legacy further.
Amen

Affirmation

As your week unfolds and starts,
remember to make decisions, guided by your heart.
When this message pings on your phone,
always remember you're not alone.
Keep on smiling and stay blessed,
it's another day of life, so don't get stressed! Amen

Hurt

Why does it hurt,
when he did the dirt.
Time should heal,
but all I feel,
is confusion and sadness,
by what you reveal.

Selfish I know,
what I reap I have sown.

My own needs, took precedence over yours,
now it is you, that has won the score.

I never thought I would feel this way... do I wonder...
what if... you stayed.

I can't shut the door, because I always want you near
Knowing you are still around, I feel a sense of unfear.

A Blessing in the Midst of Darkness

For a moment

For a moment, why did I freeze,
when something so precious has been given to me.
Worried and fear suddenly sets in,
of what is to come and how life will begin.
For the small little person that love has created,
in previous times was only deflated.
By loss through a journey that brings me to today
Allowing for joy and celebration on its way. Grateful I
am for all that is mine, which to others is minimal,
but it keeps me safe in mind.
Looking forward to what life awaits,
a new chapter with many significant dates.
The world around is falling away,
the day our child is born into the world,
I will turn to God and pray.
Thanking him for faithfulness and for unfailing Grace,
that he may never leave us and continue to guide in
faith.

Melanie Antonia

Covid world

Cries heard from around the world,
bodies of helplessness, many are hurled.
Oppression and fear taunt the weakened minds,
searching for answers, but some they can't find.
Very few lives are untouched by this pain, that this
conspiracy founded illness, brings very little gain.
Into our hearts we allow to feel sorrow, but
remember to rebuild or we will be left feeling hollow.
Don't feel lonely and don't walk alone, there is more
to each person than just skin and bone.
World with war, but with no physical fight, we need
to stand together with all our might.
One day we may reap, the divides that we create,
once was our lover, a friend or a mate.
Reach out and help ones that cry for need, humble
your minds and take heed.
Love those around you who show you kindness,
planting like seeds, that radiate greatness.
Dancing in the rain will wash away your pain,
I hope what I write, gives you hope and not vain.

A Blessing in the Midst of Darkness

Grace

Life has gifted me with many ups and downs,
some have made me smile and some have made me
frown.
There are times even now, I see failure in my
reflection... but why be so hard on myself... when all I
know is redemption.
Favour is grace and grace is God's love... I hold onto
his promise, like an elegant fragile dove.

Gratitude

In the stillness of time, we find calm and unwind,
allowing breeze to flow to reveal our glow.
Out from the depths comes subconscious thoughts,
tried so hard to bury and overcame with fought.
We sometimes lose our way... okay... but never
dismay.
We grow through the struggles, like jumping over
puddles.
The one thing I know, is that others see my glow.
When asked for the key... it's simply believing in ME.
You too will glow, I know that for sure, I knew from
when we spoke, your heart was sincere and pure.
Thank you for words of encouragement, I hold them
very dear, I will forever support your corner because I
know it's God you hear.

A Christmas reflection

On Christmas day,
we wish to say,
'Merry Christmas' to our family and friends, a time in
the year that we don't want to end.
A day to remember,
a time to relax,
and not forget the actual fact,
of why we come together and celebrate such time,
Where laughter is shared over a glass of wine.
An opportunity for some to say,
thank you Jesus for this day.
For generations past, have evolved traditions,
but what still remains is the
recognition.
For loved ones near and far,
who travel by foot or bus or car.
To spend time, enjoying this day of peace,
and where many can gather, to chat and feast.
So let's take a moment to remember right now,
this day for some, will not allow.
A joyous occasion due to a sudden loss,
or the fact they are a boss.

Melanie Antonia

Where Christmas day is just too much!
and the sadness and stress are a great big fuss.
If you know that someone will be alone,
or does not have a warm cosy home.
Call them up and tell them you care, and even ask if
they want to share,
A special day of love and festive cheer,
remembering those far and near. X

Hurting

In his eyes I did believe, but in the end it just
deceived. Lessons I've learnt along the way, but in
the end cannot stay.
Its caused hurt and pain, but still I stand, living for my
children who can't understand... Why a mother's
worth is not valid or treasured. But instead kicked
down like it never mattered.

Imperfect

The imperfectly perfect situation, is a new realm for
us both,
I pray that God carries me and keeps me afloat.
Every day, I am encouraged by his gentle spirit and
love,
through his kind loving servant, who I know was sent
from above.
We are two yet different children of the almighty
one,
brining his soldiers together in his plan, for which is
to be done.
Turning the door handle that leads to the unknown,
why am I so afraid, when devastation has previously
been owned?
Surely, we must take ownership, steps to a better
future,
and not live so guarded that we don't see any
pastures.
I trust you Lord, as everyone else abandoned me,
please reveal your love and eternity.
Very few times will I cry out to the Lord,

But right now, is time for me to armour with his sword.
Lean not on your own understanding but by the work of our maker,
for he will bless you always, for never being the taker.
Humility and kind hearts, are now rare qualities
When your soul meets another, it is not coincidently.

Unknown

I don't know how to respond; I don't know what to
say,
when I feel down like this, I want my pain to go away.
Keeping busy with my life, is not an easy escape,
but a self-pity action, that doesn't seem to erase.
A blessing to come who knows what that will be,
how I long for God's touch, to realise the potential in
me.
Silence is plenty right now and for some time more,
destiny will manifest, with hope at open doors.

Confirmation

Through God's word he reveals the truth,
the enemy would have us believe, that we
misunderstood.
But God knows our flaws and God knows our hearts,
from what and which we desire, right from the start.
Our troubles will be a thing of the past,
and by God's love enduring, we will remain steadfast.
God's blessings placed upon us both,
is because our father created his oath.
For every day we live by his word,
to never depart from it as we will go unheard.
Remain thankful daily for what he has done,
for what should not arise, shall not see the sun
Manifestation is starting to take place,
and once again, it is through God's grace.

Grace & mercy

When God places on your heart, to be there for someone,

it's only a matter of time and then you're no longer lonesome.

Encouraging and excelling together is what the almighty one above, will have us believe,

staying true to yourself and one another, to successfully achieve.

By Grace and Mercy alone, we are protected forever more,

no longer we fear decisions, that take us into the unknown.

A Blessing in the Midst of Darkness

Positive progress

Though through the motions we go along,

life has taught me to stay strong.

Do not rush and fall too quickly,

but be wise and gentle to the essence openly.

For we have both hurt and cannot fail again,

the scars too deep for us to go insane.

I want this meeting to be pure and sincere,

then only can we, appreciate God's intervention here.

For our connection goes beyond any other,

I do not want to lose this beyond any measure.

You are blessed and so am I,

together we can face the world with no need to cry.

Melanie Antonia

Movement

The turn and shift are simple gifts.

For when we learn we take in turns.

To talk and listen so our lives they glisten.

With breathing life and not taking the knife.

Making decisions to listen and learn,

combining our gifts and letting them burn.

Setting alight all that is right.

For what we are as chosen and be not like those
fallen.

Stand together for his glory and slowly, slowly telling
a story.

In all that we do, begin with clues.

Ready for the beginning and continue the Living.

God's chosen friend,

a friend unplanned.

yet we, both understand.

Why our paths they have crossed,

so we may exchange unwritten quotes.

Silently spoken, so we can see why we're chosen.

No force needed here, as to us it's plain clear.

That the gift we both have,

is to reach others who have lacked.

That desire to grow and let others who know,

why they are stagnant in growth,

when they want is the most.

Is to have peace and happiness,

be thankful and receive all the joy and gladness.

Only then can the grace be revealed to your face.

In his love and mercy, we grow,

and for that, we continue to sow.

Godly encounter

A mystery among the world.

He stands at ease in observation.

Though their eyes connect, at each same moment.

For the souls are speaking without words, without actions.

Without lust but deeper than that.

To start from the inside out, rather than the outside in.

The single touch of their hands as they entwine to belong.

Belong to one another as God sees it forever.

Faithfulness

We hold on to our Almighty's grace,

in which through our storms, we will see his face.

The troubles that come our way,

God encourages that they are not here to stay.

When our hearts grow weary and see no light,

our beloved reminds us, we are there in his sight.

Cry out and reveal, your desires unto him,

then he will strip your burdens and fulfil you to the brim.

Miracles are coming, they are there in the horizon,

dare to believe and you will live in abundance.

Thank you God, for all that you are and all that you do,

that your words resonate on our hearts, and remains our daily food.

Believing

Behind any new door awaits a new change,

it could bring joy or sadness, but we still remain the same.

Remain in doubt to the eye unknown,

waiting for signs, for us direct out of growth.

Yes, there is a moment, of should I or should I not,

if that appears, then fear is a lot.

Unity may develop or it may disappear,

but do not be dis heartened to the voice that we hear.

Time is crucial and not to be messed with,

If we believe it's God's work, then we stand and not play with.

For time is what we both have, that is our advantage,

God knows our plans and we should pray for his knowledge.

The vision

Our visions that God allows us to see,

is the very gift we long to seek.

For we are living on his forever promise,

like the rainbow that graces the sky ever eclipse.

To those who wants his riches and full abundance,

God will honour the blessed and provide substance.

Entwining two souls to recreate a heavenly place,

when they both know, it's because of the almighty's grace.

Discussions are easy talk, but where silence is present

It's God connecting the two, into ever forever essence.

Rising

The time has come for me to step out again,

living truly and nothing in vain.

Listening to the voice, misted far deep inside,

breathing so calmly, with little to hide.

Silence surrounds me, the best time to reflect,

working through problems and solving my debt.

Those who have come close to me, will start to see change,

but those who I remote, will have nothing to gain.

They will lose my future,

they will lose my trust,

those who envy – will no longer be lust.

God will have his way with me, then my time of prosper will come,

fulfilling my destiny,

allowing God's will to be done.

Amen x

Milton Keynes UK
Ingram Content Group UK Ltd.
UKHW020214141023
430515UK00010B/62